Bible Phonics
Workbook 3

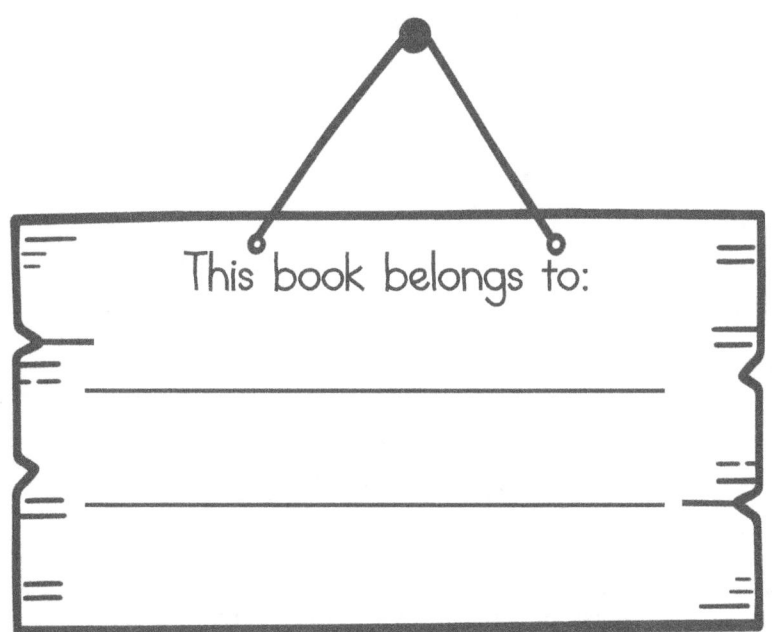
This book belongs to:

Quail Publishers

About the Series

Quail Publishers' Bible Phonics series is a revised version of the Success with Phonics series. The series includes comprehensive, high quality, Bible-based products that are aligned to English language K-2 standards. The program utilizes the Science of Reading components: phonemic awareness, phonics, vocabulary, fluency, and comprehension to ensure literacy. The explicit, systematic phonics strategies get children reading and writing from an early age, while promoting Bible principles and teachings. Each book covers a group of the most common sound-spelling combinations of the English language, with engaging, multi-sensory activities for children to read fluently and confidently.

Quail Publishers grants teachers permission to photocopy the designated reproducible pages from this book for classroom use. No other part of this publication may be reproduced, stored in a retrieval system or transmitted in any form or by any means, electronic, mechanical, photocopying, recording or otherwise, without the prior permission of the publisher.

Written by Allison Hall
Interior design by Allison Hall
Bible Illustrations by Wayne Powell
Other illustrations sourced from Pixabay, Dreamstime and FreePik. Used under license.
Bible verses adapted from the Authorized King James Version
Text Copyright © 2023 by Allison Hall
All rights reserved. Published by Quail Publishers LLC
Coral Springs, Florida USA
Email: info@quailpublishers.com or quailpublishers@gmail.com
Website: www.quailpublishers.com

ISBN: 978-0-9894627-9-2

Table of Contents

Introduction	4
Reviewing Sounds and Common Words	9
The /J/ sound	10
High Frequency Christian Word (Jesus)	12
The /V/ sound	13
High Frequency Word (have)	15
High Frequency Words (live, give)	16
The /W/ sound	17
The /X/ sounds	19
Blending, Spelling Reading	21
High Frequency Word (love)	22
High Frequency Words (come, some)	23
The /Y/ sound	24
The /Z/ sound	26
High Frequency Words (was)	29
The /Qu/ sounds	30
Blending, Spelling Reading	32
The /CH/ Sound	33
The /SH/ Sound	36
High Frequency Words (he, she)	38
The /TH/ Sounds	39
The /NG/ Sound	42
The /NK/ Sounds	44
The /WH/ Sound	45
Blending, Spelling Reading	47
High Frequency Words (me, we, be)	48
Reviewing Sounds	49
Rhymes	50
Building Words, Word Families	51
Steps to Spelling	52
The Alphabet	53
Picture Clues, Nursery Rhyme	54
Comprehension	55
Building Sentences	56
Reading	57
Alphabetic Order	58
Syllabication	59
Word List	60
Nouns	61

Introduction

Bible Phonics™ is an engaging, explicit and systematic approach to teach phonics, integrated with Bible teachings, concepts, and themes. In Bible Phonics™ A-B-C, the first book in the series, children were taught alphabetic recognition skills. However, in the second series of Bible Phonics™ workbooks, the letters are not taught in alphabetic order. The letters, **s**, **a**, **t**, and **p**, are introduced first. This phoneme sequence is used in many English-speaking countries, as it allows children to build and read words quickly and easily. Using this sequence, children can build the words: **at**, **sat**, **pat**, **tap** and **sap**, with the first four letters. Each letter is introduced with a connected Bible story to foster Bible knowledge and as reinforcement. High frequency words with irregular spelling patterns are also taught, using the **Read-Spell-Write** strategy. .

TEACHING WITH THE ACTIVITY SHEETS

Bible Phonics™ is suitable for Christian schools, churches and homes. The workbooks fully complement the kindergarten and children's Bible class curriculums. There are two reproducible pages dedicated to teaching each letter sound and its connected Bible lesson. There are also activities to help you review the sounds taught. When children participate in the multisensory activities in the books, they learn:

- **Bible Teachings:** Learn about Christ's teachings, life in ancient Israel and more
- **Phonemic Awareness**: Identify sounds in spoken words
- **Phonics:** Understand letter-sound correspondences
- **Handwriting**: Write the letters and letter combinations that represent each sound
- **Spelling**:
    * Use picture clues to complete words with the target sound
    * Identify the correct spelling of words with the target sound
- **Reading**: Read decodable sentences with words with the target sound
- **Composition:** Build sentences with the target sound
- **Comprehension**: Read decodable stories and rhymes

The pace of each lesson is always dependent on children's mastery of each letter sound and understanding of the lesson. Children should also fully understand a letter sound, before another is introduced.

Using the Bible to Teach the Phonics
<u>Before the lesson</u>

1. Review all aspects of the letter and main picture you will be teaching.

2. Read the Bible story, or connected text, and further literature on phonics.

3. Develop an exciting and engaging lesson which allows for multisensory activities and integrate technology, where applicable.

4. Make sure that children have the necessary stationery and resources to participate in the lesson.

5. Ensure lessons have activities to foster home-school connections.

6. Be aware that some children will have more advanced phonics knowledge than others. Use differentiated instruction to meet each student's needs.

<u>Teaching the Lesson</u>

7a. Sound Review – Review previously taught sounds and high frequency words with irregular spelling.

7b. Phonemic Awareness – Invite children to listen carefully as you say the sound you are teaching. Precise pronunciation, or pure sounds, should be said for all letters. Slide or bounce the sound into the picture name. For example say, /J-J-J-Jesus/. Always, stress the sound you are teaching and model the proper mouth position to say each letter sound correctly. Ask children to repeat the sound thrice. Invite them to name the letter that says the sound.

Note that some sounds are continuous and can be easily stretched (stretchy sounds), for example /v/. However some are non-continuous sounds and can't be stretched (bouncy sounds), for example /j/. Non-continuous sounds must be said at least thrice, so that children hear them clearly. Children should also be made aware that a sound can be represented by two letters, for example letters 'ch' stand for /ch/. This is called a digraph, however in a consonant blend such as **c/l**, both sounds are heard. Children should be taught to <u>sound out</u> the digraph, not the sounds of the individual letters.

8. **Phonics - Remind children that every letter has a name and a shape, and stands for a sound, or sounds. For example, letter 'J' stands for /j/, as in Jesus. Draw their attention to supporting main picture in their workbooks.** If there is a child in the class with a name that begins with the letter and sound you are teaching, say his/her name. For example, say, "/**J**/ also stands for **J**ill". Briefly discuss aspects of the main picture. For example, Christians are followers of Jesus, who is the Son of God and the Messiah.

9. **Letter Formation - Write the letter in its upper and lower case forms on the board.** Show the sequence in which each letter is formed and the proper pencil grip. Have children use the activity sheets to form the letters properly, and develop beautiful and legible hand writing.

   Use mnemonics where necessary. For example, for lower case 'j', you can say, "Make it look like a fishing hook. Draw a straight line down. Then curve to left when you reach the end". Place a dot above your line." Point out to children that letters look alike and have various shapes or font styles. For example: 'b' and 'd' are often confused.

10. **Letter Knowledge - Inform children that letter sounds can be heard at the beginning, middle and end of words.** The activities in the book allow children to further build their letter knowledge. Always read and explain the instructions to children.

11. **Reading Connection - Read the Bible story relating to each main picture to promote reading, Bible knowledge,** a sense of story, comprehension skills, and as reinforcement strategies. Ask students questions about each story. There are also sentences and short passages that children must read to apply, practice and master their phonics skills. Students should also be engaged in other interesting multicultural literature daily.

12. **Blending – As soon as children have learned the first three letters, they should be taught to blend letter sounds to read words with vowel-consonant (VC), and consonant-vowel-consonant (CVC) phonemes.** These are popularly called green words, as they are phonetically decodable. The green symbolizes 'go,' as children should read them easily. Use onsets and rimes (word families) to help children to read and spell these words quickly.

13. **Writing – Once children have learned a number of words, you should guide them in spelling, reading, and composing simple sentences.** Reinforce that a sentence starts with a capital letter and has an end mark.

14. **Reinforcement – Use songs, puppets, art and craft, and other activities to make the lessons more engaging and meaningful, integrate subject areas, and reinforce the letter and sound being taught.** Revise the letters of alphabet in sequence often.

15. **Assessment** – Use authentic assessment tools to measure students' progress

Blending Words

Blending is a very important phonics skill that children must master to read words and build fluency. Blending is the first stage in reading as letters are no longer seen in isolation. It involves sliding the individual speech sounds (phonemes) in a word quickly, in order to decode the word. Mastery of blending words improves with modeling and practice. Always model the blending process and reinforce the procedures. Here are some steps to take when blending a word.

1. Write the word 'at' on the board. Place sound buttons or dots (•) under the letters in the words. Sound buttons tell children how many phonemes are in a word. To indicate a digraph or trigraph, a line is used.
2. Point to the letter 'a' and invite the children to say its sound. Then point to letter 't' and invite the children to say its sound.
3. Sound talk the word while slowly sliding your finger under it. Sound talk is saying the sounds in the word slowly, only leaving a short gap between words. Say, a→t.
4. Do the procedure again quickly and say the word /at/. Avoid pausing between sounds. Invite students to say the word. Ask them how many sounds are in the word. Always explain the meaning of unfamiliar words.
5. Add the letter 's' to the beginning of the word, then invite children to say the new word. Place new words on the word wall. Then inform children to place it in their word bank.
6. Provide opportunities for children to work as partners to spell green words, using onsets and rimes (word families). This can be done with letter cards or tiles.

High Frequency Words

High frequency words are those words that appear most frequently in texts. These words include, '**and**', '**I**', '**is**', '**the**', '**can**' and '**to**'. Children must learn these words very early in order to read sentences automatically, accurately and fluently. Some high frequency words can be decoded easily, as they follow the regular spelling rules. However, some have tricky parts that do not follow the regular spelling rules and can be a challenge for young readers. These irregular spelled words are called sight words or tricky words or red words, as it is expected that children should *read them when they see them*. There are also some words, such as '**her**' and '**like**', that do not have an irregular spelling pattern. However, they can be taught as sight words, as children may not yet be introduced to their sounds and spellings.

Teaching Sight Words

The Bible Phonics™ program uses the Read-Write-Spell strategy to teach sight or tricky words. Here some steps to teach sight words using this strategy.

- Say the sight word being taught three times. Ask children to repeat the word twice.

- Invite children to sound out the letters in the word.

- Discuss the irregular, or tricky part of the word (*where the letter does not correspond to the sound, or sounds children associate with that letter*). For example, letter 's' can stand for /z/ in words.

- Have children trace the word, after which they will spell the word on their own.

- Write the sight word on a card and place it on a word wall. Color-code the word, to remind children of the tricky part. Children should write it in their word bank.

- Refer to the word regularly until children learn it.

Reinforcement Strategies

Word Wall
A word wall is a great tool that supports phonics instruction. It is a display of words, or word parts, that is used to teach spelling, reading and writing. Mount words with the sound-spelling being taught or sight words on a wall as reinforcement.

Word Bank
A word bank is a great way for children to improve their vocabulary, create a word list, reinforce alphabetical order and memorize the spelling of unfamiliar words. Children may use a notebook to create their word banks. Have them devote a sheet of paper for each letter. At the top of each page, they should write each letter in its upper and lower-case forms. Ensure that they start with letters '**Aa**', as the bank should be arranged in alphabetical order. Children should place new words they have learned in their bank.

Name _____ Date _____

Reviewing Sounds and Common Words
These are some common words with the letter sounds that you learned in workbook 2. Say the sounds. Read the words below.

e u r h b f l

up had him

his if of

off let tell

get big fell

run ran but

leg sell pen

red rap lot

miss kiss ill

Name _____   Date _____

The /j/ Sound

Say the picture name. Listen for the **first** sound. Say the sound.

Jj Jesus

Story Time: Listen carefully as your teacher or parent reads the Bible story below. What did you learn from the story?

Bible Story: Jesus Goes to Jerusalem
Bible Lesson: Matthew 21:1-11
Bible Theme: Jesus Saves Us

One day Jesus and his disciples left for Jerusalem. When they were near, Jesus said to his disciples, "Go into the village ahead and get a donkey and her colt. Bring them to me. If anyone asks you about it, tell them the Lord needs it."

The disciples got the animals and put their cloaks on them. Jesus rode into Jerusalem on the colt, with a large crowd following him. The people spread their outer coats on the road to welcome Jesus. They cut branches and waved them.

The people shouted, "Hosanna to the Son of David! Blessed is he who comes in the name of the Lord. Hosanna in the highest heaven!"

When Jesus reached Jerusalem, everyone kept asking, "Who is this?" The people in the crowd said, "It is Jesus, the prophet from Nazareth in Galilee." Hosanna means save us, and **Jesus came to earth to save us.**

Name _____   Date _____

Handwriting
Trace and write.

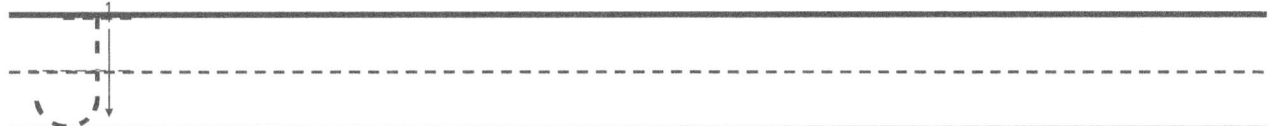

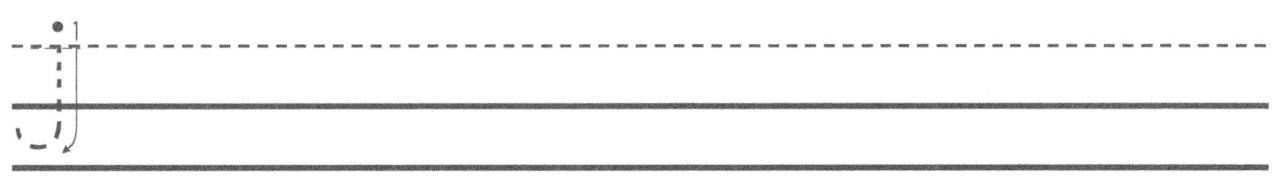

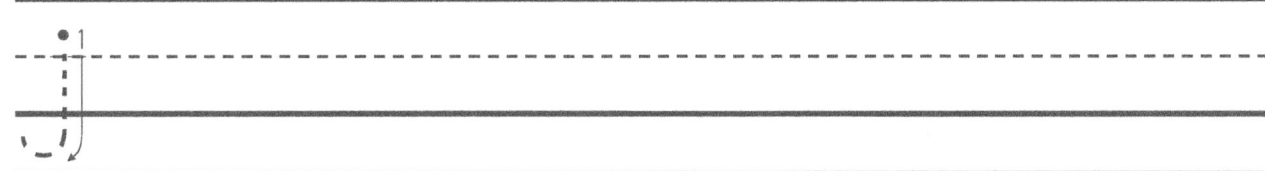

Spelling
Say the name of each picture. Then write the missing letters to complete the words.

___ellyfish   ___acket   ban___o

Identifying Sounds
Say the name of each picture. Then circle those that **begin** with the sound /j/.

   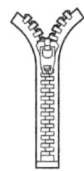   

Name _____ Date _____

 Common Christian Word

Read
Say the word.

Jesus

Write
Write the word.

Jesus

Spell
Circle the correct spelling of the word.

Jesus   Jesu   Jezus   Jesus

Trace the word 'Jesus' to complete the sentence. Read the sentence.

Ten sick men met

Jesus.

Color the word. Then write it in your word bank book.

Jesus

Name _____ Date _____

The /v/ Sound

Say the picture name. Listen for the <u>first</u> sound. Say the sound. English words do not end with 'v'. An 'e' always follows letter 'v' at the end of words.

vine

Story Time: Listen carefully as your teacher or parent reads the Bible story below. What did you learn from the story?

Bible Story: Vines in the Vineyard
Bible Lesson: John 15:1-8
Bible Theme: Share Christ with Others

Grape is a popular fruit worldwide. Grapes grow on long vines. The vines are the part of the plant that climbs or crawls. They hold the branches and give them life to bear fruit.

Jesus said, "I am the true vine. My father is the gardener. He cuts off every branch that does not give fruit. He cares for those that give fruit. He makes them bear even more fruit."

We must be like the branches of the grape tree, and remain with Jesus, the true vine. **We bear fruit when we share the teachings of Jesus with others.** This will help them to learn more about him and encourage them to become Christians.

Name _____   Date _____

Handwriting
Trace and write.

Spelling
Say the name of each picture. Then write the missing letters to complete the words.

___an   se___en   hi___e

Identifying Sounds
Say the name of each picture. Then circle those that **begin** with the sound /v/.

Name _____ Date _____

 **High Frequency Word**

Read
Say the word.

Write
Write the word.

have

Spell
Circle the correct spelling of the word.

have   had   have   has

Trace the word '**have**' to complete the sentence. Read the sentence.

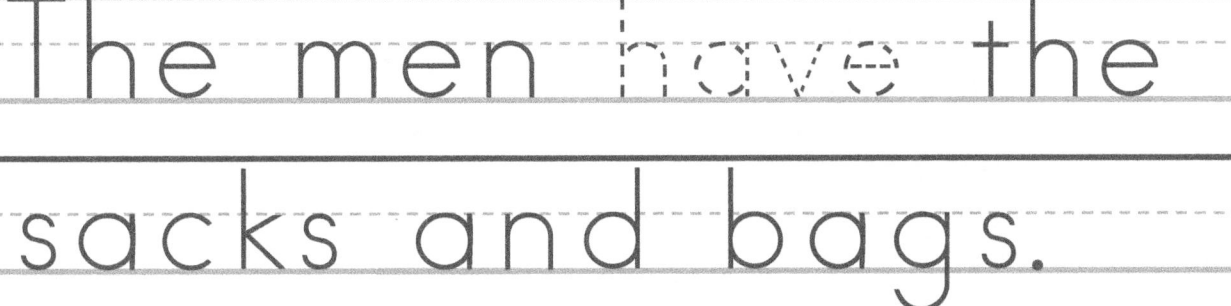

Color the word. Then write it in your word bank book.

© Quail Publishers LLC 2023 — Bible Phonics Workbook 3 | 15

Name _____ Date _____

High Frequency Words

Read
Read the words.

Write
Trace the words, then add them to your word bank book.

Spell
Write either '**live**' or '**give**' on the lines to complete the sentences. Read the sentences.

Jack and Jill _____ on a hill.

The men _____ the hen nuts.

Sentence Building
Complete the sentence below by writing the name of the city or community in which you **live**.

I live in

Name _____ Date _____

The /w/ Sound

Say the picture name. Listen for the **first** sound. Say the sound.

Ww
well

Story Time: Listen carefully as your teacher or parent reads the Bible story below. What did you learn from the story?

Bible Story: The Woman at the Well
Bible Lesson: John 4:1-42
Bible Theme: Share Your Faith

One hot day Jesus stopped by a well to rest. A Samaritan woman came to the well to get water. Jews did not like Samaritans, but Jesus loves everyone.

Jesus said to the woman, "May I have a drink of water please?" The woman was very surprised.

"You are asking me, a Samaritan, for water?" she said.

Jesus told her yes. He told her many things about herself. She was so surprised that Jesus knew all these things about her, although he had just met her. Jesus told her that he was the Messiah. The woman was so excited to meet the Messiah. She left her water jar and ran back to her village to tell everyone about Jesus.

The people in her village believed her. They came to look for Jesus. They begged him to stay and teach them. Jesus stayed with them for two days and taught them about the Kingdom of God. **We must always tell others about Jesus.**

Name _____   Date _____

Handwriting
Trace and write.

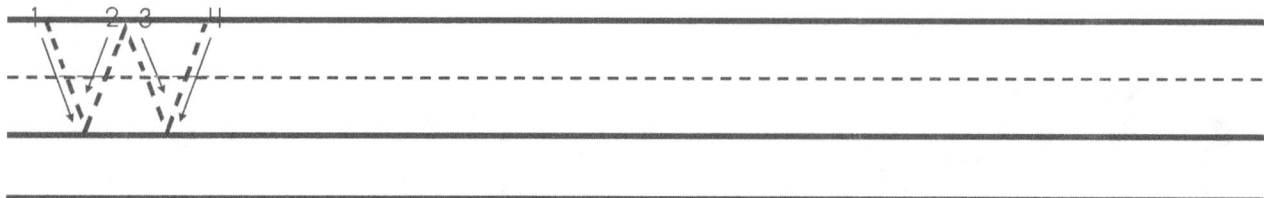

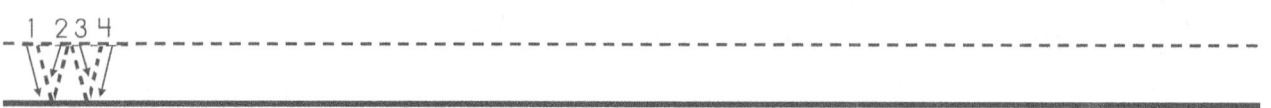

Spelling
Say the name of each picture. Then write the missing letters to complete the words.

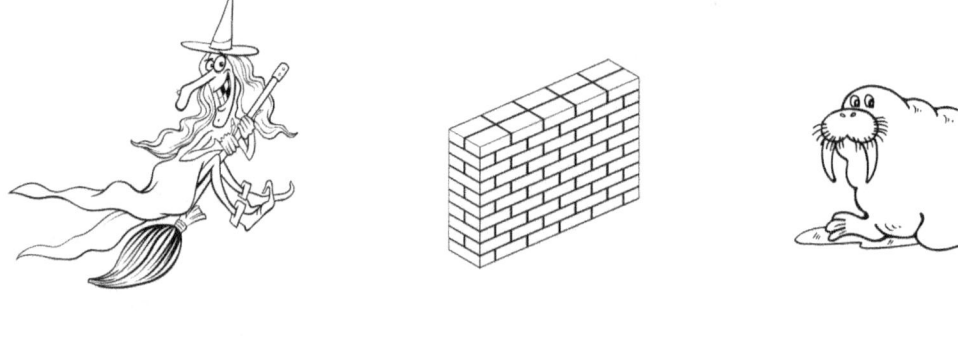

___itch   ___all   ___alrus

Identifying Sounds
Say the name of each picture. Then circle those that **begin** with the sound /w/.

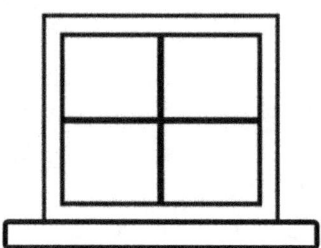  

Name _____   Date _____

The /x/ Sounds

Say the picture name. Listen for the **last two** sounds. The letter '**x**' stands for the sounds /ks/. Say the sounds.

fox

Story Time: Listen carefully as your teacher or parent reads the Bible story below. What did you learn from the story?

Bible Story: Herod the Fox
Bible Lesson: Luke 13:31-32
Bible Theme: Always Be Careful

Foxes are found in many parts of the world. Some people think they are wild dogs or wolves. However, these animals are cousins of the fox.

Foxes have long, thin legs. They have pointed noses and bushy tails. They have small bodies and move about quietly and quickly.

One day Jesus was teaching in Jerusalem. Some religious leaders said to him, "Leave this place. Herod wants to kill you."

Jesus said to them, "Go and tell that fox that I drive out evil spirits and heal people. Tell him that I cure people today, tomorrow, and the day after."

Jesus called Herod a fox because foxes are very tricky animals. They will lead other animals away to their death. Herod wanted to know where Jesus was because he wanted to kill him. **We must always be careful. There are people who will try to lead us away from Jesus.**

Name _____ Date _____

Handwriting
Trace and write.

Spelling
Say the name of each picture. Then write the missing letters to complete the words.

mi___er   si___   o___

Identifying Sounds
Say the name of each picture. Then circle those that **end** with the sounds /x/.

      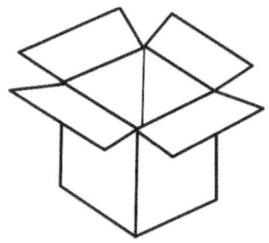

20 © Quail Publishers LLC 2023   Bible Phonics Workbook 3

Name _____   Date _____

Blending
Use sound talk to say the letter sounds in each word. Then blend the sounds to read the words.

w e t

s i x

j u g

v a n

w i l l

b o x

Spelling
Say the picture names. Then circle the correct spelling for each picture.

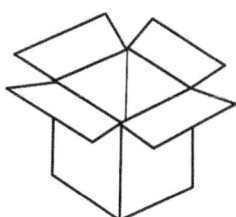

jug mug   box fox   web wet

Reading
Read the sentence.

Max and Val jog to get fit.

Name _____   Date _____

 High Frequency Word

Read
Say the word.

Write
Write the word.

Spell
Circle the correct spelling of the word.

live   love   have   love

Trace the word '*love*' to complete the sentence. Read the sentence.

I love Jesus.

Yes, Jesus loves me.

Color the word. Then write it in your word bank book.

Name _____   Date _____

High Frequency Words

Read
Read the words.

Write
Trace the words, then add them to your word bank book.

Spell
Write either '**come**' or '**some**' on the lines to complete the sentences. Read the sentences.

Jesus will _____ back.

_____ of us will live with him.

Sentence Building
Write a sentence below with either '**come**' or '**some**'.

_____

_____

_____

_____

Name _____ Date _____

The /y/ Sound

Say the picture name. Listen for the **first** sound. Say the sound.

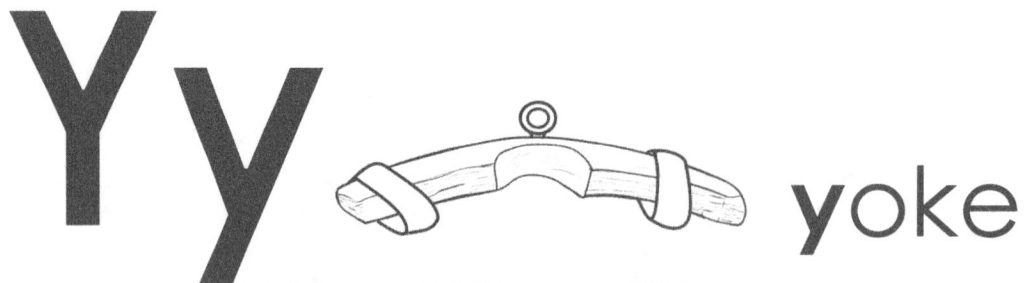 yoke

Story Time: Listen carefully as your teacher or parent reads the Bible story below. What did you learn from the story?

Bible Story: Hananiah Yanks the Yoke
Bible Lesson: Jeremiah 28:1-17
Jeremiah 29:1-14
Bible Theme: Be Hopeful

One day God told Jeremiah to wear a heavy yoke. The yoke was to remind the Israelites that they should stay in Babylon. But the Israelites wanted to go back home to Israel. However, God said that they should stay until it was the right time.

One hot summer day Prophet Hananiah told the people a lie.

Hananiah said, "God told me that he will remove the yokes from your necks soon. God will also bring back the temple treasures." The people believed Hananiah. Hananiah then yanked the yoke from Jeremiah's neck and broke it. Jeremiah told Hananiah that he was not telling the truth.

God did not like what Hananiah did. He caused Hananiah to die soon. God told Jeremiah to tell the people not to listen to prophets who tell lies.

God told the Israelites, "I will bring you home to Israel again, for I know the plans I have for you. These plans are good. They are to give you hope."
There is always hope when we follow God.

Name _____ Date _____

Handwriting
Trace and write.

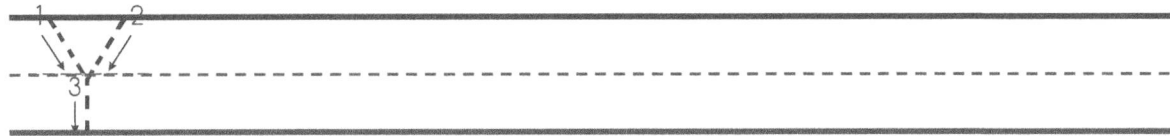

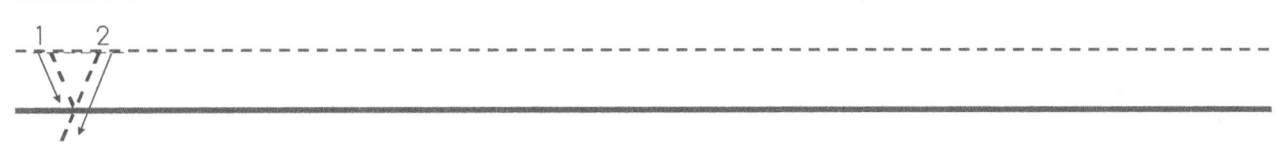

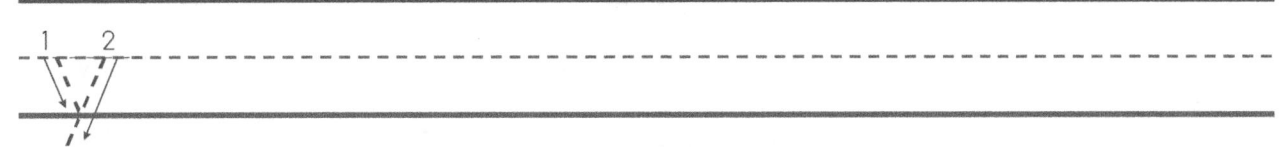

Spelling
Say the name of each picture. Then write the missing letters to complete the words.

___am   ___oyo   ka___ak

Identifying Sounds
Say the name of each picture. Then circle those that **begin** with the sound /y/.

Name _____   Date _____

The /z/ Sound

Say the picture name. Listen for the **first** sound. Say the sound.

Zz   Zacchaeus

Story Time: Listen carefully as your teacher or parent reads the Bible story below. What did you learn from the story?

Bible Story: Zacchaeus Zooms Up a Tree
Bible Lesson: Luke 19:1-10
Bible Theme: Be Honest

A large crowd was following Jesus to the city of Jericho. Zacchaeus a rich tax collector was in the crowd. He was a short man, and so could not see Jesus above the crowd. He quickly ran ahead and climbed up a tree. Zacchaeus thought that he could see Jesus better from the tree.

When Jesus came to the tree, he looked up and said, "Zacchaeus, come down quickly. I must stay at your house today."

The people did not like this. They did not want Jesus to be the guest of sinner. But Zacchaeus liked the teachings of Jesus. He was happy that Jesus came to his house. Zacchaeus was sorry for what he did to others.

"I give half of my wealth to the poor," he said. "And if I have cheated anyone, I will repay them four times the amount."

Jesus said, "Today, salvation has come to this house. For this man too, is a son of Abraham, and I came to seek and save the lost." **We must always be honest in all that we do.**

Name _____ Date _____

Handwriting
Trace and write.

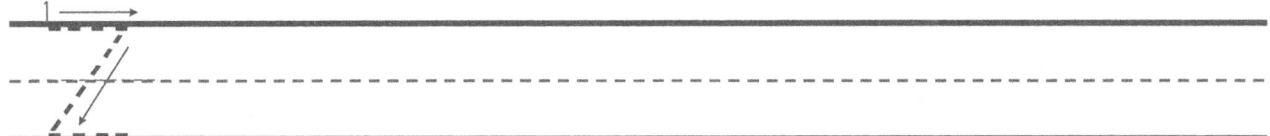

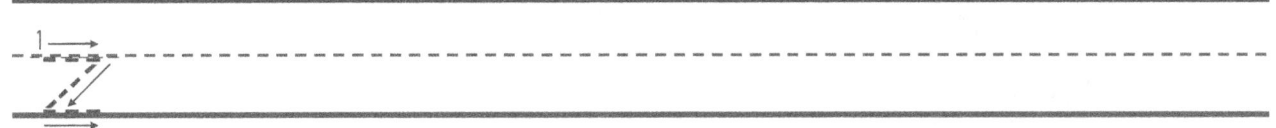

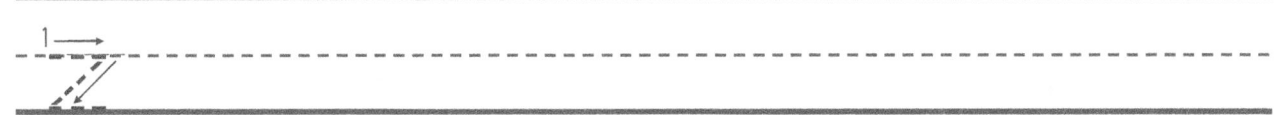

Spelling
Say the name of each picture. Then write the missing letters to complete the words.

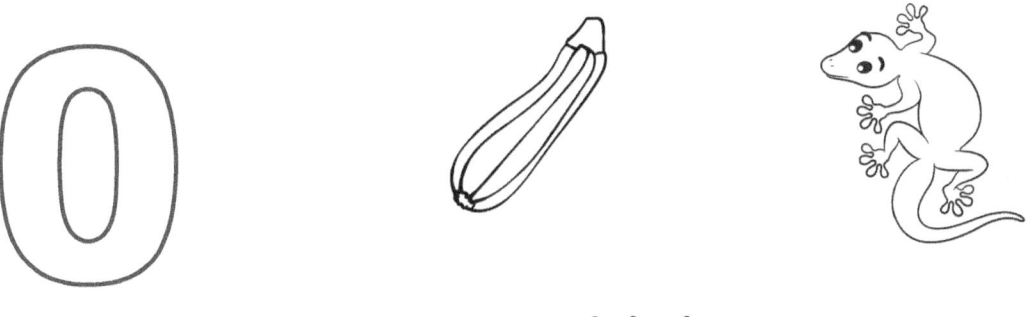

___ ero   ___ucchini   li___ard

Identifying Sounds
Say the name of each picture. Then circle those that **begin** with the sound /z/.

 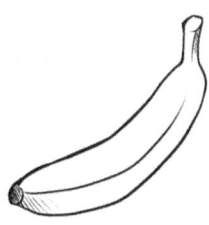 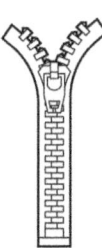

Name _____   Date _____

The /z/ Sound

Say the picture name. Listen for the <u>last</u> sound. Say the sound. The letters 'zz' stand for one sound, /z/ as in bu**zz**.

bu**zz**

Phonics Tip: When the sound /z/ is heard after a short vowel sound in a one-syllable word, it is spelled with the letters 'zz'. For example: bu**zz**.

Blending
Use sound talk to say the letter sounds in each word. Then blend the sounds to read the words. How many sounds are in each word?

buzz   jazz   fuzz

Reading
Read the sentence.

Buzz! Buzz! Is it a bug?

Name _____ Date _____

High Frequency Word

Read
Say the word.

was

Write
Write the word.

was

Spell
Circle the correct spelling of the word.

as   was   when   was

Trace the word 'was' to complete the sentence. Read the sentence.

Jesus was on the cross.

Color the word. Then write it in your word bank book.

was

Name _____ Date _____

The /qu/ Sounds

Say the picture name. Listen for the **first two** sounds. The letters 'qu' stand for the sounds /kw/. Say the sounds.

  queen

Story Time: Listen carefully as your teacher or parent reads the Bible story below. What did you learn from the story?

Bible Story: The **Q**ueen Who Wouldn't **Q**uit
Bible Leson: Esther 4, 5, 6, 7
Bible Theme: God Saves

Queen Esther was the wife of King Xerxes of Persia. One day a man named Haman told the king a lie. He said that the Jews were not loyal. Haman even tricked the king into passing a law to have Jews killed. Haman did this because Mordecai, a Jew, did not bow down to him. He was so angry that he even prepared a place to hang Mordecai.

Mordecai was Queen Esther's cousin. He quickly sent a message to Esther about Haman's plan. Queen Esther was quick to help her people. She invited her husband to a big meal and told him about Haman's plan. King Xerxes was very angry when he heard about the plan.

"Who is he? Where is he? Who has dared to do this?" he shouted. Esther pointed to Haman. The king had Haman hanged in the place he prepared for Mordecai. He passed a new law that said that Jews should protect themselves from those who try to hurt them.

Today, the Jews celebrate the holiday Purim, to remember how God saved his people. **God saves us when we obey him**.

Name _____ Date _____

Handwriting
Trace and write.

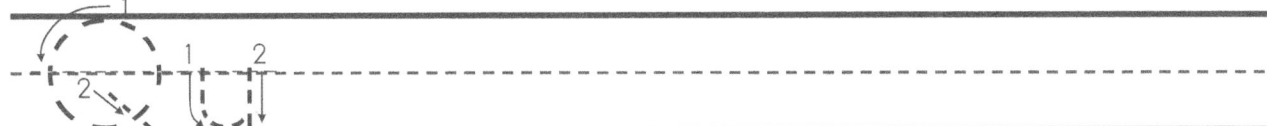

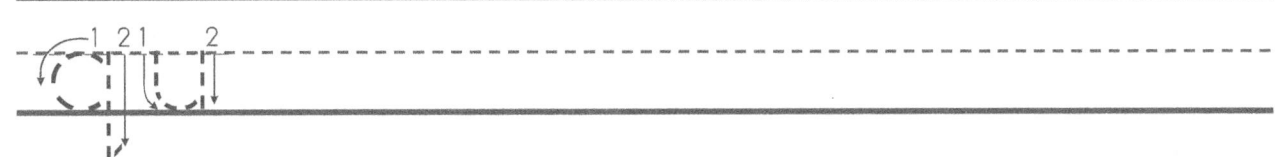

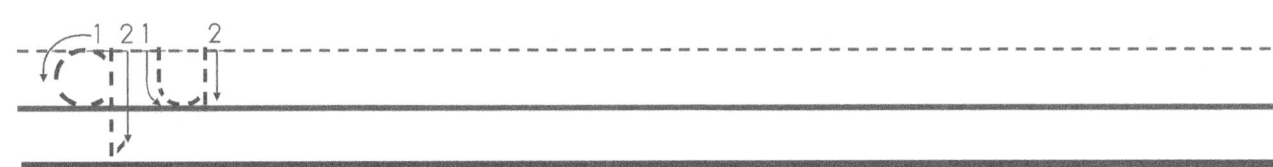

Spelling
Say the name of each picture. Then write the missing letters to complete the words.

__ __ ail   s__ __are   __ __arter

Identifying Sounds
Say the name of each picture. Then circle those that **begin** with the sounds /qu/.

Name _____   Date _____

Blending
Use sound talk to say the letter sounds in each word. Then blend the sounds to read the words.

quit   yes   yell

buzz   zip   quiz

Spelling
Say the picture names. Then circle the correct spelling that represents each picture.

   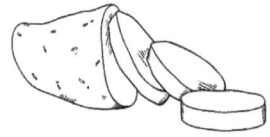   

zip zap   yam dam   quilt quiz

Reading
Read the sentence.

Zan and Yen did well on the quiz.

Name _____   Date _____

The /ch/ Sound

Say the picture name. Listen for the **first** sound. Say the sound.

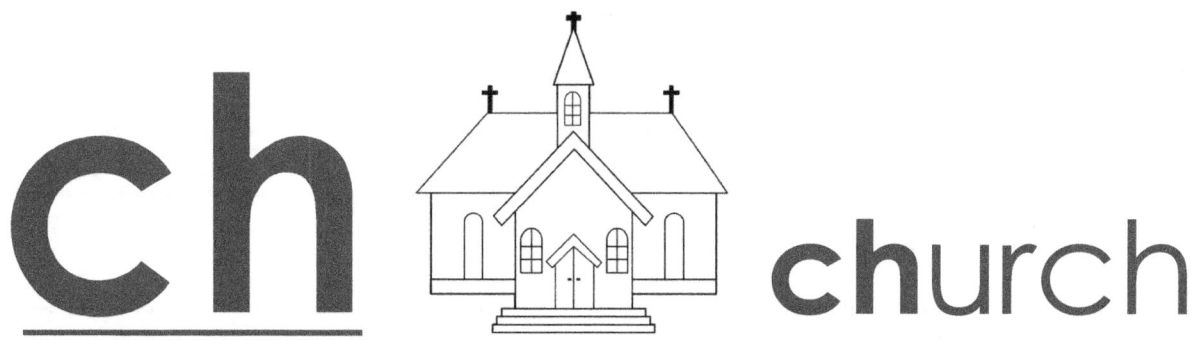

Story Time: Listen carefully as your teacher, or parent, reads the Bible story below. What did you learn from the story?

Bible Story: The Church
Bible Lesson: Acts 2:42-47
Bible Theme: Join God's Family

Do you go to church? What is the name of your church? How often do you go?

Many people believe that a church is just a building. But the Bible says that a church is a gathering of people who believe in Jesus and follow his teachings. Jesus is the leader of the church. The church is also called the house of the Lord. The members call themselves brothers and sisters.

The first Christians met in houses. They prayed, broke bread, and told many people about Jesus. They also sold what they had and shared it with others. Soon, many people became Christians.

Going to church is a happy time. There are many Bible classes, services, and exciting events for everyone. These activities help you to learn more about Jesus and his teachings.

Jesus also went to the Jewish place of worship often when he was on Earth. It is called a synagogue. **We obey Jesus when we go to church often and follow his teachings.** We should also take part in church activities and encourage others to come along.

Name _____   Date _____

Handwriting
Trace and write.

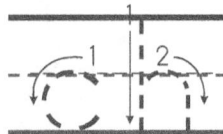

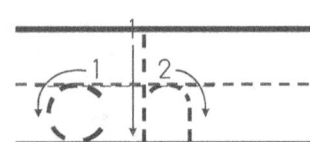

Spelling
Say the name of each picture. Then write the missing letters to complete the words.

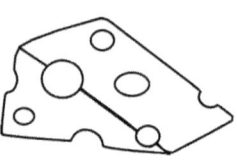  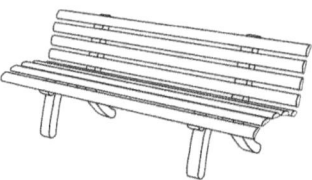

____eese   tea____er   ben____

Identifying Sounds
Say the name of each picture. Then circle those that **begin** with the sound /ch/.

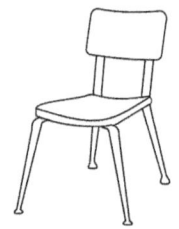      

Reading
Read the words with the /ch/ sound.

chip   chin   check

chat   much   such

34   © Quail Publishers LLC 2023   Bible Phonics Workbook 3

Name _____   Date _____

The /ch/ Sound

Say the picture name. Listen for the **last** sound. Say the sound. The letters '**tch**' stand for one sound, /ch/ as in wi**tch**.

tch — wi**tch**

Blending
Use sound talk to say the letter sounds in each word. Then blend the sounds to read the words. How many sounds are in each word?

catch   pitch   match

fetch   patch   hatch

Reading
Read the sentence.

The witch fell in a ditch.

Name _____ Date _____

The /sh/ Sound

Say the picture name. Listen for the **first** sound. Say the sound.

sh   ship

Story Time: Listen carefully as your teacher, or parent, reads the Bible story below. What did you learn from the story?

Bible Story: Paul is **Sh**ipwrecked
Bible Lesson: Acts 27:1-44
Bible Theme: God Always Fulfills His Promises

The Apostle Paul was a follower of Jesus. He traveled to many countries to tell people about Jesus. Many Jewish leaders did not believe in the teachings of Jesus and blamed Paul for causing riots. They also said that Paul was not respecting the Jewish laws and temple. The Roman officers believed them, and arrested Paul and put him in prison.

Paul was in prison for a long time. Then, one day, they sent him and other prisoners on a ship to Rome. When the ship was passing near the island of Crete, it fell into a terrible storm. Everyone was scared.

Paul said, "None of us will die. Only the ship will be lost. Last night an angel told me that I should not be afraid. The angel said that I would stand before the Roman ruler Caesar and God would save all of us."

The strong storm winds threw the ship on a rock and smashed it into pieces. All the people on the ship swam to shore safely, just as the angel promised. **God always fulfills his promises.**

Name _____   Date _____

Handwriting
Trace and write.

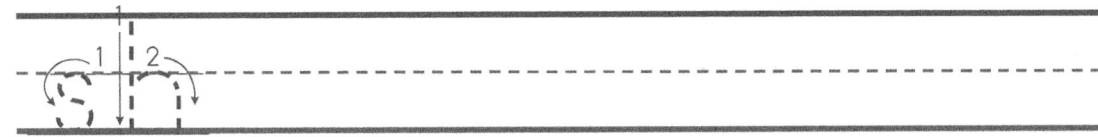

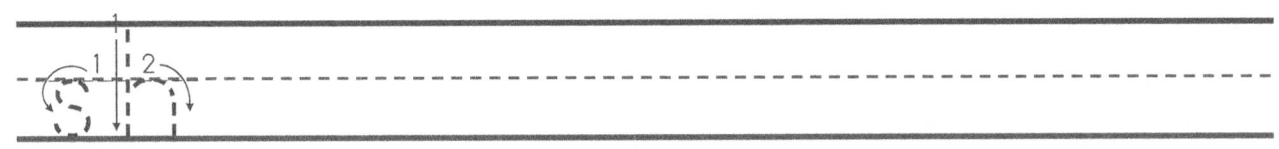

Spelling
Say the name of each picture. Then write the missing letters to complete the words.

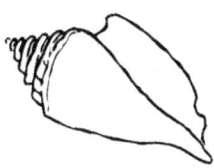      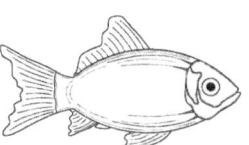

____ ell   mu____room   fi____

Identifying Sounds
Say the name of each picture. Then circle those that **begin** with the sound /sh/.

Read the words with the /**sh**/ sound.

shop   wish   shed

ship   mash   rush

Name _____   Date _____

High Frequency Words

Read
Read the words.

Write
Trace the words, then add them to your word bank book.

Spell
Trace the words **she** and **he** to complete the sentences. Read the sentences.

1. She is at the well.

2. Did he catch fish in the net?

Sentence Building
Write a sentence below with either, **he** or **she**.

_____
_____
_____

Name _____   Date _____

The /th/ Sound

Say the picture name. Listen for the **first** sound. Say the sound. This is the unvoiced 'th' sound.

th ___   thorn

Story Time: Listen carefully as your teacher or parent reads the Bible story below. What did you learn from the story?

Bible Story: The Thorns
Bible Lesson: Matthew 27:20-56
           Luke: 23:1-52
Bible Theme: Jesus Saves

Have you ever been pricked by sharp thorns? Well, that was what happened to Jesus before he was killed.

Jesus did many good things when he was on Earth. He taught people, healed the sick, and fed those who were hungry. Jesus even brought some dead people back to life. When the religious leaders saw what Jesus did, they grew jealous. They told many lies about Jesus and had him arrested.

The Roman leaders, Pilate and Herod knew that Jesus did nothing wrong. However, some of the Jewish leaders and people wanted to kill him.

The people shouted, "Crucify him! Crucify him!" And so, Pilate told the soldiers to kill Jesus.

The soldiers put a purple robe on him. They made a crown of thorns and put it on his head. The sharp thorns cut his head. The soldiers mocked him, beat him, and spat on him. They gave him a heavy cross to carry up a high hill. The soldiers then nailed him to the cross. But Jesus was not afraid to die. Jesus forgave them, as he knew that his death was to save us all. **We must always forgive others, even when they are unkind to us.**

Name _____   Date _____

Handwriting
Trace and write.

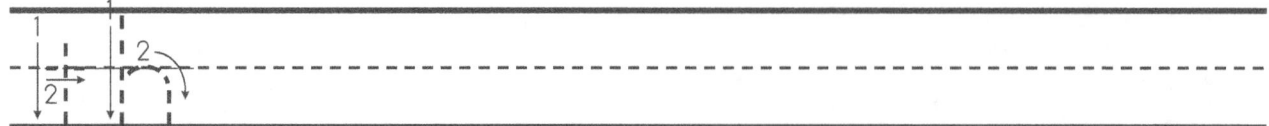

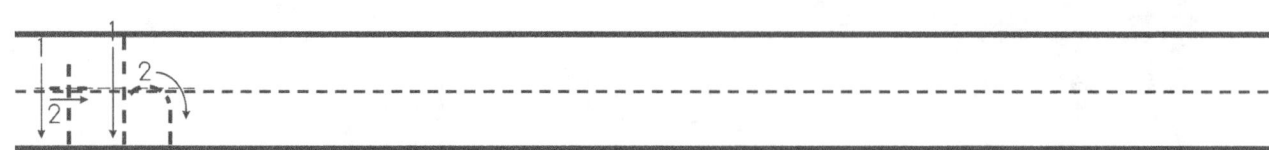

Spelling
Say the name of each picture. Then write the missing letters to complete the words.

____ ief   slo____   mo____

Identifying Sounds
Say the name of each picture. Then circle those that **begin** with the sound /th/.

3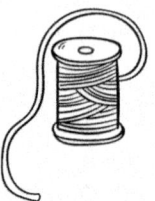

Read the words with the /th/ sound.

thin   thud   thick

with   moth   thug

Name _____   Date _____

The /th/ Sound

Say the picture name. Listen for the **middle** sound. Say the sound. The letters '**th**' also stand for the sound, /th/ as in fea**th**er. This is the voiced '**th**' sound.

Blending

Use sound talk to say the letter sounds in each word. Then blend the sounds to read the words. How many sounds are in each word?

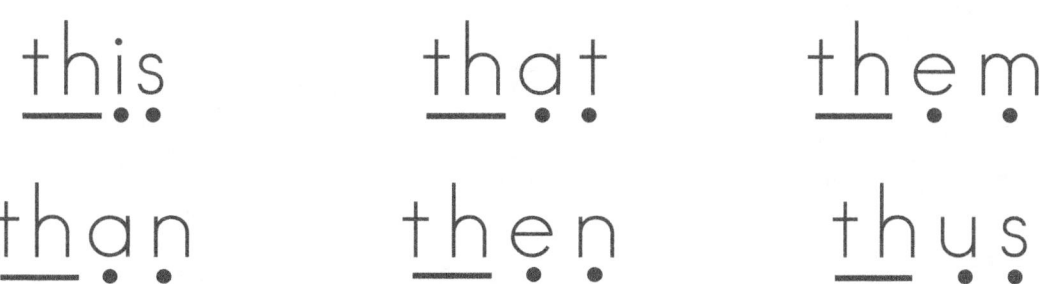

Reading

Read the sentence.

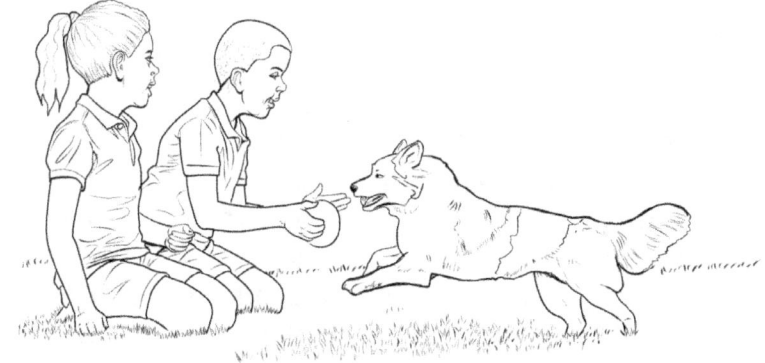

The dog runs to them.

Name _____   Date _____

The /ng/ Sound

Say the picture name. Listen for the <u>last</u> sound. Say the sound.

ng  ki**ng**

Story Time: Listen carefully as your teacher, or parent, reads the Bible story below. What did you learn from the story?

Bible Story: The King who Loved to Sing
Bible Lesson: Psalm 23
Bible Theme: Sing Praises unto God

Do you love to sing? What are some of the songs that you love to sing or hear others sing? There once lived a king who loved to sing and play his harp. His name was David.

He wrote many poems of praise called Psalms. He set his poems to music and sang them. Before David was a king, he was a shepherd boy. Many of his poems are about the beautiful countryside where he lived.

A popular poem of praise is Psalm 23 in the Bible. A part of it reads, "The Lord is my shepherd, I shall not want. He lets me lie down in green pastures. He leads me beside still waters. He restores my soul."

In some of his psalms, King David calls for God's help and forgiveness. The Bible says that we should sing unto the Lord a new song.

Good songs help people to feel happy. They praise God and tell him how they feel. They also help to share the teachings of the Bible. **We should always praise God for all he has given to us.**

Name _____   Date _____

Handwriting
Trace and write.

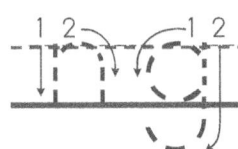

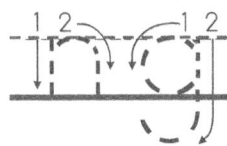

Spelling
Say the name of each picture. Then write the missing letters to complete the words.

      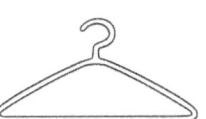

ri____   go____   ha____er

Identifying Sounds
Say the name of each picture. Then circle those that **end** with the sound /ng/.

   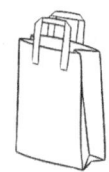   

Read the words with the **/ng/** sound.

sing   thing   song

ring   hang   wing

Name _____   Date _____

The /nk/ Sounds

Say the picture name. Listen for the **last two** sounds. Say the sounds.

nk   ink

> **Phonics Tip:** The sounds, /**nk**/ as in i**nk**, stand for the combined sounds /ng/ and /k/.

Blending

Write the letters "**nk**" to complete the words. Then blend the sounds to read the words.

bang   ba___   sing   si___

wing   wi___   thing   thi___

Reading

Read the sentence.

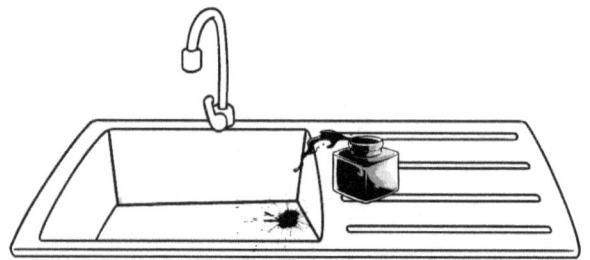

Ink fell in the sink.

Name _____ Date _____

The /wh/ Sound

Say the picture name. Listen for the **first** sound. Say the sound.

wh — whale

Story Time: Listen carefully as your teacher, or parent, reads the Bible story below. What did you learn from the story?

Bible Story: Jonah and the Whale
Bible Lesson: Jonah 1, 2, 3 and 4
Bible Theme: Obey God

Have you ever been asked to deliver an important message? Well, that was what God asked Jonah to do. God said, "Go to Nineveh and preach to the people. Tell them to stop doing bad things, or I will destroy their city." But Jonah did not like the people of Nineveh. He got on a ship which sailed off to another city.

While Jonah was asleep below deck, God sent a bad storm. The sailors were afraid. They woke Jonah and asked him about the storm. Jonah told them that God sent the storm because he disobeyed him. He told them to throw him overboard. But the sailors wanted to help Jonah. They tried to row to shore, but the storm grew worse. The sailors threw Jonah into the sea and the storm stopped.

God prepared a big whale to swallow Jonah. Jonah stayed in the whale's belly for three days and three nights. He prayed and asked God to forgive him. The whale took Jonah ashore and spat him out.

Jonah went to Nineveh and told the people what God had said. Everyone, including the king, believed him. They fasted, prayed, and asked God to forgive them. God forgave them and did not destroy the city. **We must always obey God and do what he asks us to do.**

Name _____ Date _____

Handwriting
Trace and write.

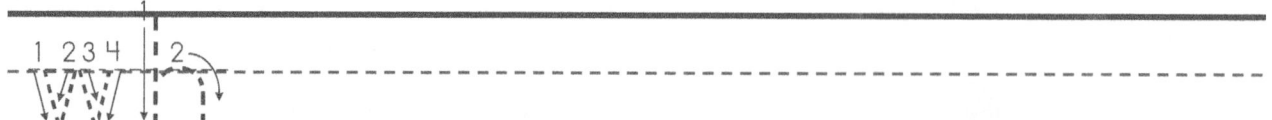

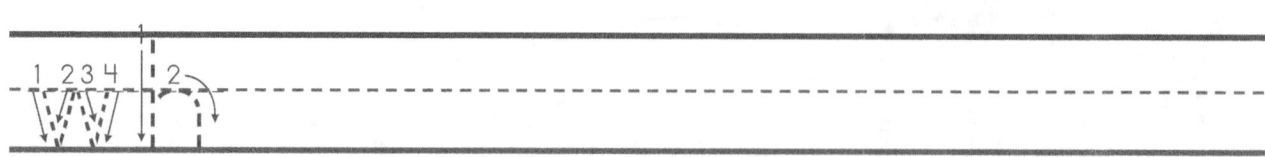

Spelling
Say the name of each picture. Then write the missing letters to complete the words.

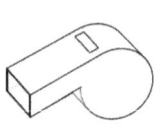 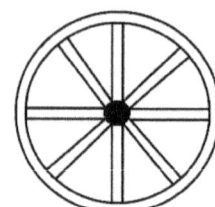 

_____istle   _____eel   _____isk

Identifying Sounds
Say the name of each picture. Then circle those that **begin** with the sound /wh/.

 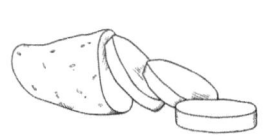 

Read the words with the **/wh/** sound.

when   which   what

whip   whiz   whack

Name _____ Date _____

Blending
Use sound talk to say the letter sounds in each word. Then blend the sounds to read the words.

whip   long   them

sing   thank   with

Spelling
Say the picture names. Then circle the correct spelling that represents each picture.

      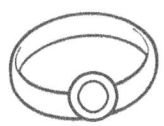

fox box   jug mug   ring wing

Reading
Read the sentence.

Chang sells fish and chips at his shop.

Name _____ Date _____

High Frequency Words

Read
Read the words.

Write
Trace the words, then add them to your word bank book.

Spell
Write either '**me**', '**we**' or '**be**' on the lines to complete the sentences. Read the sentences.

1. Jesus will _____ at the well.

2. _____ will go the well.

3. He will bless Val and _____.

Sentence Building
Write a sentence below with one of the words: '**me**', '**we**' or '**be**'.

_____

_____

_____

Name _____   Date _____

Reviewing Sounds

Beginning Sounds: Say the name of each picture. Listen carefully for the <u>first</u> sound. Circle the letter or letter team that stands for the sound.

sh   ch   wh

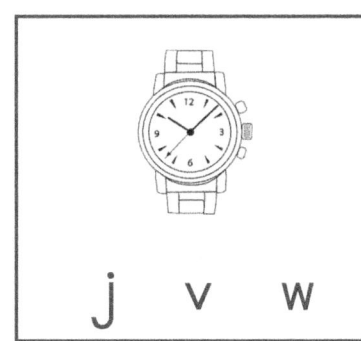
j   v   w

th   ch   qu

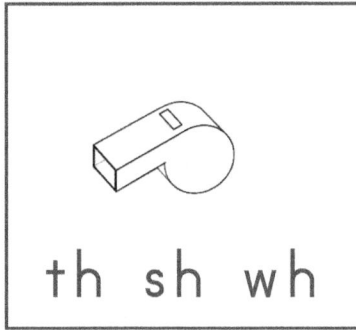
th   sh   wh

qu   sh   th

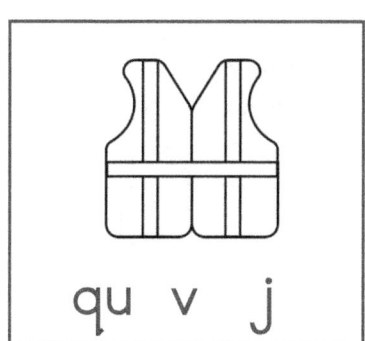
qu   v   j

End Sounds: Say the name of each picture. Listen carefully for the <u>last</u> sound or sounds. Circle the letter or letter team that stands for the sound or sounds.

th   sh   ch

ng   nk   wh

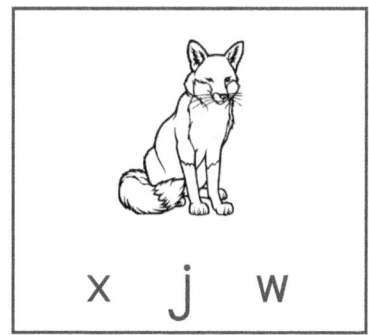
x   j   w

Bible Phonics Workbook 3 | 49

Name _____   Date _____

Rhymes
Connect the Rhymes: Read the words below. Draw a line to connect those that rhyme.

fox   mug

whip   king

ring   ship

jug   ran

van   box

Find the rhymes: Write the word from the box that rhymes with each underlined word to complete the captions.

> shop   box   sing
> fish   wig

A <u>dish</u> of _____.

The <u>king</u> will _____.

<u>Fox</u> in the _____.

A <u>pig</u> in a _____.

<u>Hop</u> to the _____.

Name _____ Date _____

Word Building with Vowels: Add vowels to complete the words. Read the new words you made. Use them in sentences.

Add 'a'	Add 'o'	Add 'i'
ch__t	j__g	qu__t
y__k	ch__p	z__p
th__nk	sh__t	sh__p
r__ng	m__th	wh__z

Word Families: Read the words. Then place them under the correct word family.

rang	mash	sang	fang
cash	dash	such	much

-ash words	-ang words	-uch ords
_____	_____	_____
_____	_____	_____
_____	_____	_____

Bible Phonics Workbook 3 | 51

Name _____ Date _____

Steps to Spelling

- **Look** carefully at each picture
- **Say** the picture name
- **Listen** for the letter sounds
- **Write** the letters that represent the sounds. Use the sound buttons (•) to guide you. Each stands for **one** sound. A sound button below a long line (‾•‾) represents a digraph (two letters that stand for one sound)
- **Read** the word that you have written
- **Check** your spelling

   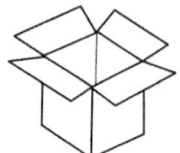   

___ ___ ___   ___ ___ ___   ___ ___
 •   •   •   •   • ••   •   •

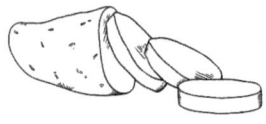      

___ ___ ___   ___ ___ ___   ___ ___ ___
 •   •   •   •   •   •   •   •   •

Guess the Riddles: Listen carefully as your teacher or parent reads the riddles below. Then write the missing letters to complete the word.

A deep hole where you get water. w___ ____

A tool used to cut and split wood. a___

An animal that lives in the sea. f___ ____

A woman who performs magic. w___ ____

Name _____   Date _____

The Alphabet
Every letter has a position in the alphabet. Write the missing letters of the alphabet in their upper and lowercase forms.

Aa   Bb   Cc   Dd   Ee
Ff   Gg   Hh   Ii   ____
Kk   Ll   Mm   Nn   Oo
Pp   ____   Rr   Ss   Tt
Uu   ____   ____   ____
____

Letter Shapes
Match each uppercase letter with its lowercase form.

J   v   X   z

Q   j   Y   x

V   w   Z   y

W   q

Name _____ Date _____

Picture Clues
Use the pictures as clues to help you to spell the missing words and complete the sentences. Read the sentences.

1. The _____ hit the rocks and sank.

2. He will wash the _____ and dish.

3. Did the _____ catch the hen?

4. A big _____ is in the net.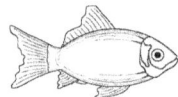

5. A fat _____ hid in the shed.

Christian Nursery Rhyme: Use the picture and <u>underlined</u> words as clues to help you to complete the rhyme. Read the rhyme based on John 4:1-42.

Ding, dong, **bell**
Jesus is at the _____.
He is with Miss **Jen**.
She runs to tell the **men**
that Jesus is at the well.

Josh runs up the **hill**.
To get Chang and **Will**.
The men get Pat and **Jem**
Then Ben, Rob and **Shem**.

Ding, dong, **bell**
Jesus is at the _____.

Comprehension: Read the passage and answer the questions.

Red Hen and the Fox

It is Red Hen. She has six chicks. Red Hen and the chicks plan to go to the mill. A sack of nuts is at the mill. But Rex the fox is at the mill. Rex gets in a big box. Red Hen and the chicks spot the fox. Red Hen will not go to the mill. She will go to the shed. Vin the bad dog is at the shed. Zack the big pig is at the shed. Rex will not go to the shed. Off he runs to the hill!

Write the correct word on the line to complete each sentence. Write the word pairs that rhyme in your notebooks.

1. Red Hen has _____ chicks.
   a. ten   b. six   d. seven
2. Rex is a _____ .
   a. socks   b. fox   c. box
3. Red Hen and the chicks go to the _____ . .
   a. mill   b. shed   c. hill

Discussion

1. Why did Red Hen want to go to the mill?
2. Why did the fox run off to the hill?
3. What is a fox? What does the Bible say about foxes?

Name _____   Date _____

Building Sentences: Read the sentence based on John 21:3-19.

The men will catch a lot of fish.

Write a sentence about the picture.

Capital Letter	Spelling	Handwriting	Finger spaces	Punctuation	Sentence Makes Sense
A	s.a.t			•	

56 © Quail Publishers LLC 2023   Bible Phonics Workbook 3

Name _____   Date _____

Reading: Read the following sentences.

The king and the witch met Sam.

The ship hit the rocks and sank.

The man hit the rocks with a rod.

We rang the bells at six.

Which kid won the match?

Vin got a cat at the pet shop.

Josh will go to the bank to get cash.

Zack has a cut on his chin.

She has a fish in the tank.

Mom will fix the hem with a pin.

Name _____   Date _____

Alphabetic Order: Place the words in alphabetic order on the lines below.

ant ✓	up	quit	dog	ink	egg
bag	man	vet	fish	ring	gum
yam	sun	jug	kit	lock	Xmas
pig	nut	cat	zip	tag	hat
ox	well				

1. ant
2. _____
3. _____
4. _____
5. _____
6. _____
7. _____
8. _____
9. _____
10. _____
11. _____
12. _____
13. _____
14. _____
15. _____
16. _____
17. _____
18. _____
19. _____
20. _____
21. _____
22. _____
23. _____
24. _____
25. _____
26. _____

Syllabication: Some words have two parts. Each part has one vowel sound.

1. Blend the sounds to read the first part of the word.
2. The blend the sounds to read the second part of the word.
3. Put the two parts together to read the word.

vel / vet = velvet

zig / zag = zigzag

cob / web = cobweb

wig / wam = wigwam

pub / lish = publish

yel / ling = yelling

sing / ing = singing

go / ing = going

box / ing = boxing

Sab / bath = Sabbath

Beth / el = Bethel

Word List: Below is a list of words with the letters and sounds taught in this workbook. The list also includes high frequency words. Read the words, then use them to build sentences.

Letter Sets	Words			
8 j v w x	+ j	+ v	+ w	+ x
High Frequency six will have* was*	jam Jill jet jog Job Jack Jen	van vat Viv vet	will win wit wag wig web	ax tax wax six mix fix ox fox box vex Rex
9 y z,zz qu	+ y	+ z	+ zz	+ qu
High Frequency yes quick	yap yet yes yell yuck	zap zip zed	buzz jazz	quack quick quit quiz
10 ch tch sh th	+ ch	+ tch	+ sh	+ th (unvoiced)
High Frequency such much that this then them thing with he* she* me* we* be*	chat chin chip chick chill check chuck such much	catch latch match hatch patch fetch itch pitch witch botch hutch	ship shop shed shut shack shock dash mash cash bash rash mesh fish dish wish posh hush rush lush	thick moth math with thin
11 th ng nk wh	+th (voiced)	+ ng	+nk	+ wh
High Frequency thank think which what when	that this then them	sang rang hang fang sing ring king thing wing song long gong sung rung hung	sank tank rank bank thank ink sink pink link wink think sunk bunk	what whip when which
Simple words with two syllables				
zig/zag = zigzag cob/web = cobweb pub/lish = publish fin/ish = finish wind/mill = windmill				

Name _____   Date _____

Singular and Plural: A noun names a person, place, animal, or thing. Some nouns are **singular**. This means that there is **just one of them**. Some are **plural**. This means that there are **more than one of them**. We can add the letter 's' to many nouns to show that they are plural, or more than one. Letter 's' can stand for the sounds /s/ or /z/ in these words.

Singular	Plural	Singular	Plural
one cat	two cat___	one cup	three cup___
one ship	two ship___	one ant	many ant___
one cap	four cap___	one bag	two bag___
one ring	three ring___	one dog	two dog___

© Quail Publishers LLC 2023   Bible Phonics Workbook 3 | 61

Name _____   Date _____

Naming Words: A noun is a word that names a person, place, animal, or thing. Select one of the letters you have learned, then write nouns beginning with the letter sound on the lines for each. Draw or cut and paste pictures in the box to show the items. Together with your parent or teacher, use a map to help you to find the name of the country, then draw its landform or shape.

The Noun Game

_____ The name of a boy.	_____ The name of a girl.
_____ The name of an animal.	_____ The name of a food.
_____ The name of an object.	_____ The name of a country.

www.ingramcontent.com/pod-product-compliance
Lightning Source LLC
Chambersburg PA
CBHW082247300426
44110CB00039B/2463